BEYOND 80

Dr. John Ayoola Akinyemi

Beyond 80
Copyright © 2024 by Dr. John Ayoola Akinyemi

ISBN: 979-8894790565 (hc)
ISBN: 979-8894790541 (sc)
ISBN: 979-8894790558 (e)

Library of Congress Control Number: 2024920369

All rights reserved. No part of this publication may be reproduced, distributed, or transmitted in any form or by any means, including photocopying, recording, or other electronic or mechanical methods, without the prior written permission of the publisher and/or the author, except in the case of brief quotations embodied in critical reviews and other noncommercial uses permitted by copyright law.

The views expressed in this book are solely those of the author and do not necessarily reflect the views of the publisher, and the publisher hereby disclaims any responsibility for them.

The Reading Glass Books
1-888-420-3050
www.readingglassbooks.com
fulfillment@readingglassbooks.com

Table of Contents

Chapter 1: My Early Life *1*

Chapter 2: High School from 13 to 18 Years Old *4*

Chapter 3: Post High School, My First Job, at Age 18 ....*7*

Chapter 4: Training to be an Agricultural Assistant at the School of Agriculture at Akure *8*

Chapter 5: College Life in America *10*

Chapter 6: Living with the Portner Family in Aurora *14*

Chapter 7: Transitioning to the Northern Illinois University, (NIU), DeKalb, Illinois for my Master's Degree ...*16*

Chapter 8: From NIU to Howard University for my Ph.D. *18*

Chapter 9: My Stint as Assistant Professor of Biology at Towson University, Towson, MD, 1974-1978 ....*20*

Chapter 10: A New Door Opens for me at the Bloomberg Johns Hopkins University School of Hygiene and Public Health *22*

Chapter 11: The IBM, New York Experience *24*

Chapter 12: My US Government Civilian Jobs for 27 Years ...*25*

Chapter 13: Retirement *28*

Chapter 14: Post Retirement Years *30*

Chapter 15: Being Street Wise in America *33*

Chapter 16: Reality of Aging Gracefully 37

Chapter 17: Way Forward: Some Reflections 41

Chapter 18: My Final Thoughts 44

Questions I am Most Often Asked 45

About the Author 47

Acknowledgments 49

This is my autobiography, a story of my life. I hope that you will enjoy it, and I pray that it will be a blessing to you. I have titled it "Beyond 80."

Chapter 1: My Early Life

I was born in 1942 as the middle child of eight siblings born to the late Joseph M. Akinyemi, and Chief Mrs. M. F. Akinyemi.

By default, I am the fifth child, meaning I have 4 older and 4 younger siblings. I am also the eighth of 27 grandchildren born to my grandmother. I cherish my parentage and the early discipline they impacted on us. We grew up in a Christian Family. Our parents taught us to respect and honor them, our elders, and our teachers. They taught us to put God first in everything we do. Every morning starts with family devotion. We read scripture from the Bible. Each one of us read a verse, and then passed the Bible to the next sibling until everybody got a chance to read the Bible. Then mother explained in plain language what that Bible passage expects us to do. Ingrained in my head is the golden rule: "do unto others as you would have them do unto you." This early discipline shaped my entire life. There is a saying: "that parents parent their children the way they were parented." My wife and I did just that! We raised our children the way we were raised. In other words, we brought them up the way that we were raised. If you were to ask them what they recall in their early years, they would probably tell you Dad and Mom started each morning and each holiday with a prayer. And they tucked us in at night to bed, read or told us a story from the Bible, etc. Dad and Mom lullabied us with a short African story, sang an African rhyme, and said a prayer, after which we jointly said the Lord's prayer." They would probably add "we are very fortunate to have parents who instilled in us a strong Christian ethic. I recall my mother telling me "A good name is more important than riches." She would detect, from my facial expression or body language, when I didn't quite understand what she had just told me, and then she would illustrate by saying: "your good name is more important than the ten shillings you got as your birthday gift from your Sunday School teacher.

I remember my parents emphasizing to us to believe in God, respect our elders, respect our teachers, value education, do your homework, and know whose child we are. They taught me to know whose son I am, and to know I am created for a reason. They taught me to follow the dictates of my mind, to know where I come from and to know where I am going. One thing that got ingrained in my mind to this day was her telling me: "have a plan, because if you don't, you are planning to fail." I learned very early in life to chart my own way. I do not follow others sheepishly. These Christian tenets formed the pillars of my life.

I attended Ago Oko Methodist School, Abeokuta, for my Elementary School. My principal was a man by the name of Mr. E. O. Lashore. I recall that in order to reach my elementary school, I had to pass by the Mortuary of a General Hospital. I was mortified. I used to hold my breath and run till I passed the mortuary. At school I was taught to respect my teachers, my seniors at school, and my elders. I was taught to be obedient; to say, "yes Sir, and yes Ma'am;", to do as my teacher says, and to learn my lessons. In those days, students carried a slate to scratch and make notes. There were no exercise books and certainly no smartphones, like we have today throughout most of America. When a teacher came into the classroom, students stand up and say, "good morning, Sir, or good morning, Ma'am." Then we'd sit down each student with a slate in hand, to take notes. We were disciplined. We learned the English and Yoruba alphabets. It is noteworthy that the English language has 26 alphabets; Yoruba language has 25! Yoruba does not contain C Q V X Z but with the additions of Ẹ, Ọ, Ṣ and G Also, at my elementary school, I memorized verses from the Bible, just as I did at home. Every Friday, pupils and teachers assembled before the principal. He then announced the protocol for the following week, for example, the hairstyle for the girls is "corn row" from front to back, or "popcorn" individual, front to back etc. You see, this was part of the English' way of making sure those girls had uniformity, and looked "good" in their uniforms. We assembled in front of our respective classroom teachers who inspected us for personal hygiene, namely if our hair is groomed, if nails are cut, if our uniforms are properly cleaned and ironed and so forth. The curriculum included scripture, (Bible reading), Arithmetic (Math), English, Yoruba, history, geography, and many other subjects.

For middle school, I attended Ogbe Methodist School, Abeokuta. My father was the principal. My experiences as "son of the principal" were harsh and cruel. I was subjected to greater scrutiny, namely, my fellow students, classmates, and some teachers alike expected me to be better, smarter, neater, and more curious compared to my classmates. I recall older classmates pulled my ear and used their knuckle to hit my head. Today their actions would be viewed as "harassment" or bullying. I just wanted to be myself; a normal and "regular" student just like everybody else.

Chapter 2: High School from 13 to 18 Years Old

I attended Methodist Boys High School (MBHS) in Lagos Nigeria from 1955 to 1960. My principal was Mr. S. Ade Osinulu. Before him was Mr. A. B. Oyediran, AKA "A.B.O." My class of 1955-1960 was the first and last to spend six years in high school. Prior to that, students spent five years in high school. Remember this is how the British educational system differs from most other systems, including America's. The curriculum included physics, chemistry, biology, English, English literature, Religious Knowledge, Latin, mathematics, additional mathematics, i.e., calculus, history, geography and Yoruba. During my high school years, our science laboratories were scantily equipped: we had a few Bunsen burners, Petri dishes, etc., We performed a few experiments and remembered things by rote memory. It is noteworthy that the "Old Boys," meaning previous graduates of MBHS who are in the USA, did rectify this situation by providing funding from the Old Boys Association (OBA) in North America (MBHSOBANA). Through the generosity of these Old Boys, MBHS science laboratories now enjoy modern laboratories.

I remember my physics teacher, a man by the name of Mr. M.J. Etuck. I remember my English teacher, a man by the name of Mr. G. C. Vale, He was a tall, lanky Englishman, who, I believe, was a graduate from either London or Oxford University, United Kingdom. My English Literature teacher was a man by the name of Mr. Barnes, a graduate from a University of Ireland. My Yoruba teacher was a man by the name of Mr. Olumuyiwa, whom students affectionately called "Caesar." All I recall was he was "entrepreneurial" in his own unique way. He "instituted" a "fine" for students who did something wrong, for example, reported late to class, or students who didn't conform to a certain protocol. Such students paid a "fine." The fine was kept in a locked box and at the end of the school term and school year, monies collected were turned into buying much-needed supplies or equipment for the school. I remember my Latin teacher, a man by the name of Mr. Kujore, who reportedly became a professor in one of the universities in Nigeria. He made learning Latin "declension" so much fun, almost like music. I can still hear the Latin words which mean I love, you love, he/she loves, we love, you, plural love, they love for a Latin verb "a more", which obviously means to love. My Religious Knowledge and Mathematics teacher was my maternal Uncle, the late Mr. D.O.S. Soremekun. These were my mentors. They were people who inspired me to say to myself "when I grow up, I'm going to be like them." Attending MBHS was life altering and transformative for me. It was there that I learned to appreciate dualism between excelling in sports activities and scholastic abilities. Each of us students were allocated to a "Sports Team." There were four of them, namely Westminster, Didsbury, Kingswood, and Handsworth. It was there that I learned the importance of teamwork and healthy competition to excel in life. A great many "Old Boys," i.e., graduates of MBHS continue to this day to make significant contributions throughout the world, including the founding of MBHS Old Boys Association in North America (MBHSOBANA). I had great admiration for the principal, Mr. Osinulu. I remember to this day one of the very few Latin phrases he said while addressing an assembly of us students in front of him. He said: "I am your "in loco parent is," meaning I serve as, or in lieu of, your parents; translated, if you attend this school, and you are under my watch, I am your parent. He had a passion for his students even after they had graduated. Such passion is rare but needed. It reminds me of a true dedication to his calling and duty. That Principal died at age 101, a life well lived. The MBHSOBNA responded by showing their eulogy, sympathy, and monetary gift to the family of their beloved principal. Another fun memory I had was of the principal that preceded him. As previously mentioned, his name was Mr. Oyediran (AKA "A.B.O"). All I heard from older graduates, including my oldest brother and two of my cousins, was their testimonies to his brilliance, discipline, and commitment to scholasticism.

Chapter 3: Post High School, My First Job, at Age 18

My first job after high school wasto work at the Secretariat, at Ibara, Abeokuta, my hometown, the capital of Ogun State, Nigeria. Literally, Abeokuta translates "Under the Rock." This geologic structure is called "Olumo Rock." It is a historical symbol of the Egba People, to which I belong. It is a thriving place for visitors to this day.

"My immediate boss was a man by the name of Mr. Oladigbo. One of my duties wasto assist him in reviewing Agricultural Gazettes from the United Kingdom farmers and agricultural institutions from other countries, including Egypt. This assignment opened my eyes to "think "outside the box". For example, I learned how to order 50 one- day-old chicks from Israel. All 50 of them survived! To my surprise and amazement. I then hired a local carpenter to build a wooden poultry cage for the chicks, and he did, after many reminders. I was 18 at the time and he was much older. He probably thought "what does this boy know"; hiring a 40 something year-old to work for him? That was the mentality in those days. Suffice it to say that I had so much fun watching those chicks develop into beautiful, brown-feathered chickens, which became the envy of the neighbors. They "feasted" on most of my chickens! That did not deter me. I had so much fun with that adventure.

Chapter 4: Training to be an Agricultural Assistant at the School of Agriculture at Akure

Akure is a city in Ondo State, Nigeria. It took me about 12 hours to travel by local transportation from Abeokuta. The school of Agriculture was established by the government of Western Nigeria to train Nigerians and neighboring countries including the Cameroons, West Africa and Ghanaians, and neighboring countries. It was opened to both men and women, ages 19 to 60 plus. I was paid a full salary to attend this two-year course leading to a certificate as an agricultural assistant (AA.) The curriculum included agricultural engineering, soil science, crop management, piggery, poultry, and several other agricultural subjects.

Upon satisfactory completion, students may further their training, if selected, to train in another two-year course leading to a certificate as agricultural Superintendent (AS). Students may end up attending the university to obtain their BS degree in agriculture. This qualifies them to be hired as an Agricultural Officer, (AO). From there they can be promoted to higher ranks, such as senior agricultural officer, and principal agricultural officer in the civil government.

While in residence at the School of Agriculture, I was provided housing free of charge. I had a Raleigh bicycle which allowed me to go to various farm locations on the property, which is arguably 1100 acres or more. I and fellow students attended lectures in a big hall, after which we dispersed into various field groups for practical assignments, such as animal husbandry, where I learned how to manage and observe health, diseases, and behavior of cows. I observed indentured workers who were not educated beyond eighth grade milking cows and taking care of pigs in the piggery. I learned a lot from watching these indentured workers adhere to strict health and sanitation protocols.

My weekends were free from obligations. Weekends were easy when vendors such as tailors literally invaded the campus soliciting men to have their suits custom made for them. I didn't personally like this because you have literally a sea of look-alike men's suits! I did not like to wear suits that made me look like several men on campus. I suppose this is a reminder of what I had learned, namely "be yourself, don't follow others sheepishly," etc.

Another thing I did not like was a lack of practical training especially in agricultural engineering. I did not appreciate the fact that I did not have a chance to operate a tractor, let alone hook up a tandem tractor or cultivator hooked behind that tractor. Emphasis was on rote memory to learn the parts of a tractor rather than to drive the tractor to cultivate/harvest the farm. I remembered someone telling me: "lead, follow, or get the hell out of the way. "I started thinking "get out and seek training outside of Nigeria." I saved all my money to prepare for my overseas adventure. I did not want to go to Europe; I thought of going to Israel mainly because my big boss at the Secretariat at Abeokuta, had encouraged me to study agriculture at Tel Aviv, Israel, where he was from. I applied for admission into American University at Tel Aviv, Israel as well as other universities overseas. However, thanks to my first cousin, the late Dr. Samuel O.A. Soremekun. I am eternally grateful to him for encouraging me to apply for admission to Aurora University; from which he had graduated four years earlier, in 1959. He had paved the way for my admission because he had done exemplarily well there. He completed four years of college in three years and got enviable excellent grades. Imagine how proud he made me feel during the first formal welcoming of new students with all faculty members saying to me "so, I understand you are Sam Soremekun's cousin.?" "Yes, I am," I beamed back. He was well liked by everybody, professors and the Registrar of that college, the late Dr. Clyde E. Hewitt, a Ph.D. in Historiography. I owe a great deal to my cousin. He talked to his mentor, Dr. Hewitt, of blessed memory, who helped me gain admission into Aurora University.

Chapter 5: College Life in America

I left Nigeria for the US in July of 1963. I spent late July to August of that summer with my first cousin, Dr. S.O.A. Soremekun, in Hamilton, ONTARIO, Canada. From there I traveled on a greyhound bus to Aurora, IL to start the school year. Getting to assimilate to a different culture was my first challenge at Aurora. I lived on campus for four years. I had a room to myself at Wilkinson Hall which was, and still is a residence hall for men. I shared a common large shower room with my fellow mates; so, I quickly learned a lot about human gross anatomy. That was the first time I ever saw a white man fully naked. It was their first time to see an African man butt-naked also! That was my first time seeing diverse genitalia. I saw diversity long before the use of that term became popular and common in our contemporary application to racial or ethnicity of human beings. At Aurora College, in the early 1960's, students on each floor of the dormitory shared a large common bathroom, approximately 30 feet by 30 feet, equipped with 12 or so shower heads so that twelve students can take shower at the same time, I recall the first day I ever saw snow. It was very early in the morning. My first class started at 7:30AM.I packedmy booksinmy hand,stepped out of my dormitory, clearly and totally unprepared for what I was about to see;snow all over the place. That was my first time seeing snow! I slipped and fell. My books scattered all over and I experienced a hot flash all over my body as I stepped out. Up and until that time, all my life, I had lived in a tropical climate. The shock of stepping into this beautiful white snow must have literally "electrified me." It literally and figuratively "set me on fire." In that brief moment that I fell, I experienced a heat sensation. Fortunately, some of my white colleagues rallied to gather my scattered books. As previously mentioned, I lived most of the four years on campus. I had three meals per day at the college dining hall. I quickly learned I must be there to eat at posted hours; or I would go hungry, as I did, that first semester when we changed the clocks in fall and spring. I learned a lot; "fall backwards, spring forward" respectively. I never again missed any meals for not being punctual. I arrived on time at posted mealtimes! At the college cafeteria, I also observed a lot, including why certain students would not sit by me at the dining table, or when they do, some of them would abruptly leave. I knew it was not B.O (body odor) because my cousin had briefed me to use deodorant every day. I wondered why the same students wondered why the French professor, Dr. Vanda Srouga, PhD, from Lithuania, would sit next to me while Agnes and I, and some other international students tried to practice the few French sentences we had learned from her. I wondered why some students would literally move from the table, make snaring gestures as if a fly had gone into their nostrils, etc. I wondered why some students have their last names as White, Brown, Long, Rice, etc. I said to myself: "of all the names in the Bible, why would a parent name his/her child so-and-so, like Long, or Lang, or Rice. I wondered why students a little younger than me were bald headed at age 18 or 19! I wondered about American English and the true meaning of what my college students were saying tome. Please note: up until this time I had been used to "saying what I mean and mean what I am saying." Now when I hear some colleagues of mine say to another "I'll beat the crap out of that guy", I get lost at what they meant. I recall one Thanksgiving when the college registrar, the late Dr. Hewitt had invited me and some other foreign students to dinner. I recall as I was leaving, I had thanked him for the sumptuous dinner, and he said to me "we are glad to have you. Come back again." Lo and behold, I went back tomy dormitory room and after one hour, I showed up at his house! I was being obedient to his spoken word! I wondered how my college friends looked so much alike on campus during my first two semesters.

I could never tell who Craig was or who John was. They all looked alike to me. Interestingly, CraigBailey, DanDobbert, Ray Spangler, and JohnBorick became my lasting friends. I am sure they in turn wonder what I was speaking about and some ridiculed me by saying "I can't understand you.

What are you saying? You speak British English. I don't. Talk normal to me, what do you mean? Talk regularly". And then deep down I wonder whether he had meant to be engaged in a broil with me in the first place! Oh, so much fun understanding each other! It was at Aurora university that I met a young lady from Kenya, East Africa. This young lady ended up as my wife of almost 50 years. I wrote and published a biography named Coming 2 America. Her biography is a testimony to her undying love, persistence, and perseverance. I encourage you to read this amazing biography of her life.

College life remains my best life. If I must do it over, I would not change much. I reminisce on what it means when brilliant students surround me. I quickly learned how to search for a "purpose in life", and how to build on that purpose once you find it! I owe a great deal to my mentors, my professors, and lasting friendships I made through college.

Colleges were "empty" though, during college breaks, especially for "foreign students" who have nowhere else to go when their college mates go home to celebrate the holidays with their families during Easter and Christmas breaks. The dormitories close during those holidays. Out you go! If you are lucky enough, you may have a friend invite you along to visit their family. If you are not, you are out in the cold. A property owner is not keen on renting you a room for two weeks, you cannot afford a hotel room! It is brutal. Sometimes you pick up a phone to call property owners if they have a room to rent. Sometimes you would show up, and they would tell you the room that they said was vacant ten minutes ago is already rented to somebody else. The only difference is now they see your face! I am extremely grateful to Adib Dagfall and his wife, Halla, for hosting Agnes at their "married students" hostel during one Christmas Holiday at Quonset barracks at Aurora College campus.

I recall my first Christmas. My girlfriend, whom I had befriended from the School of Agriculture in Nigeria, prior to both of us coming to the US, invited me to visit her at the Florida Agricultural and Mechanical University (FAMU) in Tallahassee, FL. I traveled on the Greyhound bus from Aurora to Tallahassee FL. Prior to going to Florida my college mates had warned me not to go there. Why not, I ask? They said if you a black student you may not like what you see. Sure enough, while I was in Tallahassee, FL., I saw for the first time a sign "For Colored Persons Only" posted to restrooms. I spent time at the Men's Dormitory. At least it was warm there in Florida compared to chilling weather in Aurora IL. On the following Christmas, Christmas of 1994, I was extremely fortunate to experience one week of the Christmas Season at the high elevations of Estes Park, Colorado. The natives refer to it as "Mile High." I was one of twenty-five international students who had their expenses paid to spend the holiday at Aspen, the mile-high Town, in Colorado. It was part of a program called "Experience in International Living." There we shared experiences from diverse cultures and different countries. I recall one young lady from Asia, who told us: "in my country girls don't go on a date one-on-one." In my country when I marry, I marry the whole family. Can you imagine ten to twelve people in a van on a date?" It was there in this Mile High resort that I learned the effect of altitude on making tea and breathing normally. It was there that I learned that different cultures prepare their meals similarly. For example, Iranians and Pakistanis cook their rice no differently than Nigerians or Kenyans. It was there that I learned nations are more similar than dissimilar. In other words, different nations have more in common. It was there that I learned people from diverse nations have the same "human emotions." It was there that I learned there's more that unites us than divides us.

Chapter 6: Living with the Portner Family in Aurora

    I consider this as a divine intervention. I say that because a lady had called the Dean's office asking if they knew of any international student who was willing to live with her in Aurora, Illinois. The Dean's Office gave me her telephone. I called her to tell her I was interested, and she came to pick me up from my dormitory at Aurora College, IL. She lived at 523 Batavia Avenue. She introduced me to her father, Mr. Grover Portner. She told me what my duties would be if I decided to take the job. The job was that I would take care of her father, who had one leg amputated; I would wheel him in his wheelchair around the house, bathe him, help him dress up, and help him get back to his favorite chair to watch football, which he loved. I also would occasionally watch his favorite sports with him. In return, Marjorie Portner would furnish room and board free of charge and take me to my summer job at Caterpillar Tractor Company across to the adjoining town of Montgomery, IL. Marjorie worked at Copley Memorial Hospital, a local hospital during the night shift, and return home at 8:00 in the morning. Then she took me to work. My duty was to take care of her father when she was at her night duty. The experience was very memorable and rewarding. It was a solution where everyone benefits. It lasted for many years after I had graduated from Aurora. Even when I decided to go to the Northern Illinois University (NIU) in DeKalb, IL., which is about an hour and a half drive from Aurora, she wanted me to live with her and commute to DeKalb. I respectfully declined this offer because I didn't want to take the risk of driving in winter to my classes. I ended up having an arrangement with the Caterpillar Tractor Company, or Armor Dial Company, two companies I had worked for in the past. The arrangement was that they would call me to fill in for their employees who might not show up for their night shift. I knew I could handle and schedule my classes around if I had to work the night shift on "an as needed basis." My work schedule would mean they would call me as soon as they found out there was a "no show" for the night shift. I, in turn, would drive to Montgomery IL, where Caterpillar was located. That was how I financed my way to earn my master's degree from NIU.

Chapter 7: Transitioning to the Northern Illinois University, (NIU), DeKalb, Illinois for my Master's Degree

I shared a 3-bedroom apartment with roommates from Pakistan, India, and Iran. I learned and quickly realized how similar our cultures can be. I quickly learned to marvel at things that unite us regardless of where we come from. I came to realize that for all our diversity, basic things such as the emotions of mankind are the same. We have the same fears and the same faith. Fear is "what if." We fear "what if I fail my exam?' What if I don't get that job?' What if my car doesn't start in winter?' Faith is "What Is? What is the purpose of life?"

I scheduled my classes to begin at 10:00 AM. I figured I would support myself with the night job at Aurora and be back in time from my laboratory or my classes at 10:00 AM. It worked fine. I do however notice a sharp contrast between attending a small college like Aurora and a large population of students at a university like the Northern Illinois University, (NIU), which at that time had a student population of at least 35,000 compared to Aurora of less than one thousand. Unlike Aurora, the faculty to student ratio is very low. At NIU, I was just a number. I knew I had to work twice as hard to succeed. And to do that I must discipline myself and remain focused. That came easily. I was more mature than I was at Aurora University. It was there I met a young lady by the name of Sharon. She was in her early twenties as an undergraduate student. In fact she did invite me to her wedding in Peoria IL. She got married at age 20. The summer of 1968. I attended. Then we lost contact with each other for 40 years! In 2018, she got in touch with me via letter. She had all the time been wondering whether I had returned to Nigeria. She had wondered whether I was affiliated with one of the universities in Nigeria. My family do not believe someone could still remember me after 40 years! That friendship has lasted to date! I recall my major Professor was a man by the name of Dr. Von Zellen, a graduate PhD from Duke University, North Carolina. My other Professor was a man by the name of Dr. Graves. I had another mentor, a man by the name of Dr. Hess. I am who I have become because of them. I am eternally grateful for their mentorship.

Chapter 8: From NIU to Howard University for my Ph.D.

Up until this time I have attended white colleges. This is my first experience in the US to study at a Predominantly Black University (PBU University.) I am extremely blessed that I studied at the most prestigious Howard University. Talk about living in the nation's capital; talk about a lofty experience where I was mentored by accomplished professors; talk about the first day I heard one of my major professors while I waited patiently outside his office for my opportunity to introduce my self personally to him. I have no clue who he was;I knew there was a 50:50 chance he could be white or black by the intonation of his voice. I had heard him from the outside. He was talking to somebody else on the phone. Up until this time I have not had a black professor with such an enunciation. When I was ushered into his office, imagine how elated I was to see a person who looked like me on the very top of his renowned career as a scientist. We talked for a while. I did predoctoral research under him. He was the Head of the Zoology Department. However, my PhD advisor was a man by the name of Dr. David Richard Lincicome, PhD., a world renowned parasitologist. He retired at the end of my first year at Howard University. It was there I obtained my PhD degree. It was there that my wife obtained her master's degree. The President of Howard University then was a man by the name of Dr. James E. Cheek. He was a very personable man. I was so impressed by him that I entertained writing a book and dedicating it to him. I, and a close friend, had determined to do this project. Unfortunately, Dr. Cheek passed away and I never got a chance to pay my last respects to him. My friend, Tony Mendis, who later earned his MD degree from Howard had toyed with the idea of entitling the book as "Cheek to Cheek." Dr. Cheek had a brother, also by the name of Dr. Cheek. We thought it would be appropriate to dedicate the book to the Cheek Brothers, hence, our provisional title of the book "Cheek to Cheek."

The National Institutes of Health (NIH), Bethesda, MD.

I worked the night shift in clinical pathology, where I met outstanding professionals like Dr, McLowry, MD, Dr. Zierdt, and Ms. Esther Williams. My duties included culturing pathogens, such as bacteria in the laboratory by plating them in various culture media from patients and logging them for reporting to attending physicians. Three of us graduate students worked this night shift; namely my wife, Agnes, myself and another graduate student, whose name, I believe, was Tom, or Ted. Agnes and I earned enough to support us through Graduate School.

I used the NIH library to conduct a literature search for my PhD thesis. During those days there was no internet; there were no Google searches. I had to peruse volumes of research work that other scientist had published in medical and scientific journals. That was a blessing and an honor! I poured through hundreds of scientific literatures. I made notes on my index cards with appropriate citations of who was the original scientist. This was a tremendous help in writing my thesis for my PhD dissertation.

Chapter 9: My Stint as Assistant Professor of Biology at Towson University, Towson, MD, 1974-1978

I served as an Assistant Professor of Biology from 1974 to 1978. The University terminated my contract in 1978. I was 36 years old at the time. I was at the peak of my career. I had a wonderful family of four. This termination presented me a lemon!

I will share with you how I turned this lemon into lemonade. This was a lesson I had learned from someone who said to me "when somebody gives you a lemon, turn it into lemonade and celebrate." And that is exactly what I did. I did not get stuck when I lost my job. I knew losing a job is not losing a life. I patted myself on the back knowing that in those four years I had served in that position, I had done something to mold and encourage students that came under my tutelage. I had great ravings from students I had taught. I took courage knowing I have contributed to their lives, and educational development. However, in academia as well as in politics, there has always been, and will always be issues relating to race, and opportunities for the disadvantaged members of any society. I was the only Black Biology department faculty member at Towson University. I was fully cognizant of subtle discriminations that exist. I resolved not to make my attitude ruin my altitude I comforted myself knowing that when a door closes another opens. Usually, the door that opens is bigger and better than the one that just closed behind me. I counted my blessings, namely a beautiful family of two children and my lovely wife always cheering me on and telling me go, go, go! I reminded myself of the words of my favorite pastor, the late Reverend Dr. Schuler, of Crystal Cathedral,

Orange County, California. He wrote a book, entitled, "Tough Times Don't Last But Tough People Do." I decided and knew that tough times will not last forever. I was one of those tough people.

Chapter 10: A New Door Opens for me at the Bloomberg Johns Hopkins University School of Hygiene and Public Health

By the end of summer of 1978, I gained admission into the Bloomberg Johns Hopkins University (JHU) School of Hygiene and Public Health to study for a Master of Public Health (MPH) degree program. It was there at the JHU that I met extremely brilliant men and women from all parts of the globe. These men and women were sponsored to study there by their various governments. The JHU continues to be a world class leader in science and medicine. It was there I learned how an institution like the JHU has contributed to improving World Health. The most personal experience I had was when my major professor, Dr. Morton Corn, said to me: "Now that the graduation is over, what are you doing to secure a job? I told him I had sent some resumes out and I am hopeful of landing an appointment very soon. He motioned me to come into his office, saying "let us chat for a while." Then he picked up the telephone, a Rotary dial, and called one of his contacts at the International Business Machine (IBM), in Tarrytown, New York. I heard him say "I have a young student here. He has a good head on his shoulders. He went through our program and got his MPH degree from JHU. He is trained as an industrial hygienist and an occupational safety manager through our program. He is in my office now talking to me. Can you use him at IBM in your Industrial Hygiene and Safety program?" I could not believe my ears when I heard "yes" from the other line. I thought I was going to pass out! "Can you send him so we can see him and interview him?" I bounced like a rubber ball to the ceiling! I could have hit the ceiling and bounced back when I heard this! The conversation led to "how soon can he come?" As soon as tomorrow, I shouted in excitement, but first let me talk to my family and that I will get back to you later tonight. I got home, told Agnes and the kids and I called Dr. Martin Corn, who in turn called IBM that I am willing to catch the earliest plane from the BWI airport Baltimore to JFK airport in the morning. And I did just that.

Chapter 11: The IBM, New York Experience

I flew to the J.F. Kennedy International Airport, (AKA JFK) in New York, where I rented a rental car and drove north to Tarrytown, NY. At Tarrytown, the IBM Safety Office interviewed me. They gave me a tour of the facility in their safety office. "We surely can use you. When can you start." I exuberantly and politely said "thank you; yes, thank you; please let me go home to Baltimore and tell my family. Tentatively, I can start on the following Monday. That was Friday when I said that. To cut the long story short, I started working for IBM that Monday and the rest is history. Now I truly understand the saying: "it doesn't matter what you know, it matters who you know" in this business of seeking jobs! I had a wonderful experience collaborating with a staff of three, namely an MD, a safety officer, and an industrial hygienist, in a collaborative evaluation of IBM workers Occupational Safety and health hazards and designing and recommending how to prevent workers' exposure to occupational hazards. I was hoping that I could have a permanent employment with IBM; however, I understood the pecking order, by which I mean people who have established seniority have the opportunity to compete for, and usually end up being selected to fill openings throughout the company. And that was cool with me. However, I thoroughly enjoyed the opportunity to work for IBM, the leading manufacturing industry in America!

Chapter 12: My US Government Civilian Jobs for 27 Years

On January 7, 1981, I started as an Environmental Scientist at the United States Army Toxic and Hazardous Materials Agency (USATHAMA), at the Army Aberdeen Proving Ground, Aberdeen, Maryland. After leaving there, I worked for the US Army Environmental Hygiene Agency, (USAEHA). That Agency later changed its name to the Center for Health Prevention and Preventive Medicine, (CHPPM.) I worked as an Industrial Hygienist at AEHA. From there I worked at the Kirk US Army Health Clinic (KUSAHC), and rose through the ranks to a Supervisory Industrial Hygiene position.

My next U.S. government position was with the Headquarters, United States Marine Corps, (HQ,USMC) located in Arlington, VA. That was a very fascinating job. A very challenging job and I thoroughly enjoyed working with the Marines. One of the notable work ethics I noticed with the marines is that it is an organization that truly depicts what marines are and what they do: hence they are referred to as "the few, the strong, the proud marines." I am honored to serve them as a Civilian. They treated me well. The US Marines is a fine organization. They gave me a chance to manage their Industrial Hygiene Program and to participate in their Inspector General (IG) Inspection Program. They gave me a chance to travel around the world, not only in the USA, but to Okinawa, Japan! There, at the Headquarters Safety Division, HQSD, I had a chance to work with a fine group of men and women, including my boss, by Mr. Al Lilli bridge, who retired a year ahead of me in 2005. I should note that I collaborated with exemplary men and women in the Safety Division. Noteworthy individuals include Ms. Emily Copes, who served as Secretary, and Mrs. Anna Marie Pratt, who managed a specialized aspect of the Safety Program for the marines. Both ladies remain remarkably close friends till today. I valued their friendship over the years.

 I commuted to the HQ, USMC, Safety Division located in Arlington, VA from my home in Bel Air, Maryland. This meant waking up at 3:30 AM Monday through Friday, driving my car to the Baltimore Washington International Airport, (BWI), taking a commuter train from BWI to the Union Station in Washington DC, and taking two metro buses, namely the blue line and the red line to the Pentagon Station, and taking a bus up the hill from the Pentagon to the Navy Annex. The Navy Annex is just a stones throw from the Pentagon. I had scheduled a meeting at the Pentagon the day the plane hit, on "911". Now that I looked back, I am eternally thankful that the meeting did not take place that day. However, we witnessed the entire world change on 911. The plane shook our building as it crashed into the Pentagon. Like a bad dream, the entire world witnessed an event which changed the world as we know it today. Two of my co-commuters on a commuter train lost their lives that tragic day as well as over three thousand lives. America will never be the same. Indeed, the world will never be the same after 911. The following Sunday, I went to the Bethel AME Church in Baltimore. The Pastor, the Reverend, Dr. Frank Reid, read Psalm 46: verse 1: "God is our refuge and strength, a very present help in trouble." By that time, I had lost it! I could not contain myself. I could not restrain myself. Persons sitting next to me on the pew had to hold me and restrain me! I heard them comfort me, saying "that is all right; Our God is still in control." I heard them loudly and clearly, but the emotions weighed on me, as though a heavy steel beam of the church suddenly fell on my shoulders. I had lost my composure, knowing that I could have lost my life had I attended that meeting at the Pentagon that Monday of 911. I struggled and trembled to desperately control myself. I felt somebody patting me tenderly on the back. I felt the way a baby would feel under the comfort and assurance from his mother that all will be well. God is still in charge! I shook uncontrollably. I sobbed with tears. Suddenly, I remember the shortest verse in the Bible: "Jesus wept. "That offered me wholesome comfort. Just imagine for a brief moment; I could have been one of those whose lives were instantly wiped out like the 3,000 plus lives that were lost at the Pentagon on 911.

Chapter 13: Retirement

I remember a wise man once told me "John, do not wait till you are 64 before you plan to retire. Plan to retire the day you get your first permanent job." He sounded overly full of BS; you might say; however, I said he was full of wisdom. I ask him, "how do you do that?" He said to me, "Live on the salary you received the first time you got a promotion," bank the money you receive when you get subsequent promotions. Put money away for a rainy day. So, not to brag, I adopted the wisdom of his words. My wife puts money away every time we get promotions. We tried to live very conservatively. We ask ourselves; do we really need this thing that we want to buy? Do we really want it? Or do we need it. In other words what will happen if we do not have what it is that we wanted to buy in the first place? Will it change our lifestyle? These questions help us decide on the priority of our expenses. Each of us had the benefit of retiring after serving the government for more than 25 years. To prepare for retirement, we availed ourselves with valuable information given to us by the US Office of Personnel Management, (OPM.) The United States OPM provided us with valuable information regarding health benefits and the MEDICARE system that would sustain us during retirement, and contribute to a happy, and enviable retirement. We are incredibly grateful for that. As previously stated, I retired after serving the government for over 27 years. My wife did the same.

Permit me to make a few observations regarding retirement. Retire when you listen to that inner voice that tells you this is the right time to retire. Then follow the dictates of your mind. And when you do retire, make sure you are physically, mentally, and spiritually ready for it. Do not ever think that now that I'm retired, I'm going to sit down and watch TV. You must be physically active. Sedentary life is a sure way to die sooner than expected. Immerse yourself with activities that you genuinely enjoy; perhaps you should immerse yourself in a hobby that you have long neglected or postponed? Do them now that you are retired. Ironically, keep busier than you have ever been when you had that 40-hour workweek. You are now your own boss, but do not tell your spouse or significant other that, that is what John Akinyemi said I should do. Do not get me in trouble with Momma! If you know what I mean!

Chapter 14: Post Retirement Years

It has been 16 years since I retired. I remember as I drove away from the Navy Annex in Arlington Virginia. It all seemed like yesterday; so, permit me to indulge you to travel with me as a passenger. Pretend that you are a passenger in the car. I am the driver. Enjoy the ride. I looked back through my rear view mirror. I saw a picture reflecting the Navy Annex as I drove away from it. I saw the image of the Pentagon looming massively as I drove past it. I head north to the Beltway. I reflected on an utterly unique experience I have had serving the military as a civilian. I traveled worldwide: I visited and had the chance to interact with our marines. Doing so gave me a tremendous opportunity to observe their devotion to duty, honor, and valor. Tell a Marine to wear a certain Personal Protective Equipment (PPE); they will wear it; not asking for further explanation. "Yes, Sir." In sharp contrast, based upon my experience at the Department of the Army at Aberdeen Proving Ground, tell a soldier the same thing, who would ask you "why I had recommended he wears such a specific PPE. Then, I would explain to him:" that in order for me to determine your exposure to your workplace occupational health and safety hazards, I ask you to wear this PPE and cooperate to be personally assessed. Based upon your cooperation, I will monitor your breathing levels, and recommend to the Colonel, a method to either engineer the hazard out, or significantly reduce or minimize your exposure to this and future hazards. What a contrast in the work ethics between a soldier and a Marine. "Semper Fi!" Thank you to our troops defending our freedom.

Now that I have retired for 16 years, permit me to share my reflections with you. Spend more quality time with your friends and family members. My older grandson was born six months before in the year that I retired. He is now 16 years old going on 17. In two years, he will head to college. That is how fleeting time can be. Post retirement presented and unleashed my freedom to get up whenever I want, do whatever I want to do without imposing any time constraints. I tell the people I have all the time in the world to do anything I want to do. I am now my own boss. I no longer have to commute long hours using three forms of transportation, namely: drive and park my car at the BWI train station, take the Amtrak to the Union Station in Washington,DC, take the Red and Yellow Lines to the Pentagon; then either walk up the hill, or wait for a Marine shuttle bus to the Navy Annex. On any typical workday, my total round trip commute and workday consisted of 12 to 13 hours from Bel Air, MD, to Arlington, VA., Post retirement gives me an opportunity to think about what really matters most to me. I find ample time to reflect, pray, meditate, and reminisce on God's amazing blessings. I find time to be an author to write books and share my experiences with a hope that reading my books may instill something in the minds of the readers, particularly the younger generation, as well as future generations and their family members.

To those who aspire to be an author of a book, permit me to say a word of advice: Don't hesitate to share your faith with others. Leave a legacy for your family. Hopefully, you would have taught them to know who they are, whose child they are. Hopefully you have taught them to believe in God; not to take "no" for an answer; and to have the courage to tell somebody who might say to them "you can't do that" to respond with a resounding "yes I can," a phrase popularized by the former President Barack Obama, who, in fact gave it that title, "Yes, We Can."

Since I retired, I have written and published a biography honoring my late wife. You may get it on the Internet or wherever books are sold. It is entitled "Coming 2 America." It's an incredible story of a 15-year old girl who came legally to America in search of education and a better life. I am currently writing my own autobiography, entitled "Beyond 80." If all goes right, it will be available before Christmas 2024 from local bookstores. At retirement, I developed a framework of mind which says a glass of water is half full, or half empty; it's all about one's perception. Like David, the Psalmist, and I quote: "My cup "runneth" over;surely mercy and goodness shall follow me all the days of my life and I will dwell in the house of the Lord forever." Hello, somebody. Hallelujah. Praise the Lord! Every day I wake up is a blessing. I see beauty all around me: the birds that sing, the flowers that bloom, the butterfly that delights itself with the nectar from my flower garden and pollinates my vegetables. At beyond 80 years of age, I can still dance, I can still garden. I can cook, too! The bottom line is whether you fail in life or succeed it is all a matter of your own perception and attitude. Folks, let me remind you that your "attitude" in life determines your "altitude." Dream big. Soar like the American Eagle. Don't settle for the turkey!

Chapter 15: Being Street Wise in America

I made some important observations while I was in college at Aurora IL. I noticed that diction, the way my colleagues say things is a lot different than what I had been exposed to. For example, there is a sharp difference in the meaning of words they say to me. Now that I reflect on what they are trying to tell me, I get it. Prior to coming to America, I had been taught in the British system: to speak the "King's English (maybe I should have said Queen's English!) I think you know what I mean. Speak "proper "English. I was shocked when I heard someone quite knowledgeable and educated say "there's four in my family, or "there is two reasons why I disagree with you, etc. I was taught back home in Nigeria to say what I mean and mean what I say, grammatically of course! It gets even more dramatic in the world out there, away from the college campus, when you walk on the streets of America. Here are some examples. When I moved to the nation's capital, Washington DC, I was approached one beautiful Saturday afternoon. I had parked my Volkswagen Beetle and made sure I locked the car. I was approached by a woman who said to me "are you sporting?' I replied: "yes I play soccer." She shouted some obscenity, and then said "do you want some pussy?" I said to her: "I used to have a cat when I was growing up in Africa!" She cursed me out and went on her way!

At a factory job in Aurora, a young beautiful white lady (who *so* obviously liked the way I talked), asked me to show my right palm to her. I did. She said to me "I like your nice soft hand." Mind you, I only showed my right hand. She hadn't even touched me yet! Then she said, "I would like to break your cherry." I had no clue what she was talking about!

I went downtown Washington DC on another day for a haircut. Some lady approached me and asked would you like the "p" word. This time I was smart. I replied "not only no, but hell no!) I quickly went away! That's how I became "street wise" in America. I saw a college mate downtown Aurora one Saturday and beamed at him calling his name. He ignored me as if he didn't know me! We lived in the same dormitory! When I got back into the dormitory and saw him, I didn't have the nerve to ask him about his strange behavior. Both of us felt awkward!

I must admit my shortcoming also. For example, during my freshman year, all my college friends looked so much alike to me. I couldn't tell Peter from Paul; so, to hide my "ignorance" I always smiled when they talked to me. However, I observed that they talked fast. They expected me to follow their lines of reasoning most of the time. I always thought they used a lot of American jargon and lingos that I wasn't familiar with. Obviously, they probably didn't understand me or my British accent either. I noticed though that they always complimented me by saying I talked so funny "I could listen to you all day long even though I don't understand a word you are saying."

I hear the question "where are you from"? I respond by asking them? Originally? "Yes, originally, they would say. "From my mother's womb." Some would venture to ask "but where, what country was your mother when you were born?" Nigeria," I would answer. Most of them would respond "that's what I thought. A few have asked me "where's that?" South or North Africa? I tell them neither. Nigeria is in West Africa, it is the most populous country in Africa. Some get fascinated. Some, especially a few African American ladies take a step back. I watch them take a deep breath, not knowing that I was noting what their body language was saying to me,then read their lips "OMG" (which I later learned translates as "O my God!" I had so much fun! For my first two years in USA, I carried with me a small notebook in which I wrote the real meanings of American colloquialisms, or American lingo. Previously, I mentioned how I was invited by the college registrar to his house my first Thanksgiving at Aurora College. We had a sumptuous dinner. I thanked him and his wife. He said, "we are glad to have you, John." However, as I proceeded to the door to return to my college dormitory, he said tome "hurry up, and come back." I did precisely that! I showed up at his door 90 minutes later! I was obedient to his order! I had learned from my "British" teachers back home, to mean what I say and say what I mean. Obviously,I expected the same from my professors in the USA. However, this was not always the case in America. I had a real problem and struggled deciphering meaning, intent and context of the way Americans use the English language. Especially when I took American history, one of a few required courses for graduation. To me, it seemed that I was at a huge disadvantage because my fellow students, who obviously were native born American citizens, knew what the professor was talking about. He was talking about their own history. As a "foreign student" from Nigeria,I had to learn who John C. Calhoun was, and what he did in American history. To them, it was a cup of tea and cake. Although now, after 40 plus years, I appreciate and love living in America. I feel very comfortable and very appreciative of American history. Back then though, in the mid- 1960s, I had difficulty with American History. As a matter of fact, it caused me to graduate late from Aurora College in the summer of 1967. The irony of this is, as I reflect on the many blessings I have had, I am absolutely convinced that America is the only country in the world where a "nobody", like I, coming from a "land of empty", relatively speaking,to a land of "plenty", namely the United States of America, can become a "somebody." America has offered me far more opportunities than I ever dreamed of. This nobody became somebody! As I reflect on these, let me repeat what guided me through it all.

Know Who You Are. Know whose son, or daughter you are. Believe in God; Believe in Yourself Do not Take "No" for an answer; challenge yourself to say "Yes, I can do that seemingly impossible task,so help me God. "Develop a mindset that says, "my glass of water is half full, not half empty." I dare you to go even further to say, like David, the Psalmist: "my cup runs over; surely goodness and mercy shall follow me all the days of my life." I am convinced that in life, whether a person fails or succeeds it's all a matter of his or her perception. At beyond 80 years of age, I still remember what my mother told me decades ago: "son, have a plan for your life, for if you don't have a plan you are planning to fail." I remember hearing my mother say to us during our daily morning devotions "I can do all things in Christ who strengthens me. Another favorite Mama impressed on us her children is "As for me and my house, we will serve the Lord."

Chapter 16: Reality of Aging Gracefully

I include this chapter because I think it illustrates my personal reflections of what it means to be "old" in life, and most certainly in America today. It is best summarized in Psalm 71, which is sometimes referred to as the psalm of old age. David, the Psalmist says: "for thou art my hope oh Lord God; thou art my trust from my youth." I discussed my early years in chapter one. Psalm 71, verse 6 says: "but they have been holding up from the womb thou art he that took me out of my mother's womb thou art he that took me out of my mother's bowel. "My place shall be continually of thee." I addressed this also in chapter 1. Verse 7 of Psalm 71 says, "I am a wonder onto many but thou art my strong refuge."

Many people wonder how a 21-year-old from a "third world country" can come to America and end up working at the prestigious National Institutes of Health (NIH) graduating from top-rated institutions of higher learning and retiring after 27 years of service to the nation's military. Yes, "I am a wonder unto many" all right. I am a wonder unto myself, too: but God is faithful. He remains "my strong refuge.! I tremble at God's Amazing Grace to me and my family. Verse 8 says: "Let my mouth be filled with high praise and with thy honor all day." That's why I wrote this autobiography. I want to share God's faithfulness to me. The Great American poet, Maya Angelou, wrote "why does the caged bird sing?" I challenge you to an old gospel hymn with the following refrain: "I sing because I'm happy; I sing because I'm free his eyes are on the Sparrow, and I know he watches me." YES. HE does!

Verse 9 gets more serious. It portrays a modern-day secular trend that I observed in America. Let me explain. The Psalmist in verse 9 says: "Cast me not off in the time of old age; forsake me not when my strength faileth." In America, we tend to glamorize youth and seemingly ignore our senior citizens, who have reached the age of being classified "Senior Citizens." I observed that without intentionally doing so, we put some of our Senior Citizens. We pay them little or no attention. Most often they have a limited or fixed income. Yes, I know what I am talking about. I am one of them! Many of our Senior Citizens are trying to decide whether to pay for their prescription medicines or forgo their meals. I observed that sometimes we tend to make no eye contact with them, let alone wish them good morning on the street! Let me tell you of a tribe in South Africa. A popular greeting when these tribesmen meet is a greeting which translates "I see you." A proper response is "I am here." In this Tribe, their culture is that their youth learn to NOT IGNORE their Senior Citizens! They believe that if they don't have eye contact with people in general, or with their senior citizens, how do you gain from their wisdom? I believe we need to recognize that the youth we glamorize today will soon become the senior citizens of tomorrow. We need a change of paradigm: the senior citizens we tend to neglect subconsciously or unintentionally are here to stay. Where they are we will be. We will all get there! It is not a matter of "IF; it is a matter of WHEN." So, be more mindful of senior citizens you encounter. Verse 10 says "for my enemies speak against me, and they lay wait for my soul take counsel together…" Yes, in this world you will have enemies: people who are jealous of you; jealous of your husband; jealous of your wife; jealous of your accomplishments, etc., sometimes they will band together. They will try to diminish you or minimize you because deep down they're trying to hide their insecurities.

    I experienced these emotions at least three times thus far in my life. Firstly, at Howard University where a fellow who had obtained his PhD a year ahead of me suddenly assumed a position vacated by a PhD professor under whom both of us had studied. Secondly, at another university where the faculty decided not to renew my contract as assistant professor after four years. In short, that institution fired me! How did I react? I figuratively brushed off the dandruff on my impeccable Navy-blue suit. I kept going. I could have chosen to tell myself "This is it; I am a failure; I lost a job I had prepared for all my life, etc." But again, thanks to my parents who had taught me "when life throws a lemon at your face, turn it into lemonade, and celebrate!" When a door closes behind you, a new door opens; that door is usually wider, with greater opportunities." Before that summer ended, I gained admission into the Bloomberg Johns Hopkins University School of Hygiene and Public Health for my Master of Public Health (MPH) Degree! Like Momma had taught me, I turned my lemon into lemonade and the rest is history. Many great opportunities opened to me in America. Thank God I didn't take "no" for an answer. Again, thanks to Momma. This is my tribute and testimony. I believe in God. I know who I am; I know whose son I am, and I believe I can do ALL things through God, who strengthens me. I had learned from Mom (AKA Mama), that in life, there will be troubles. But march on! Like a good Marine. That passage says, in part, "trouble may last through the night, but joy comes in the morning." Mama taught me: "In life you will suffer pain; in life, you will fail more often than succeed. Do not fret failure. Learn from it; if nothing else, you have learned how not to repeat the mistake. That's a valuable lesson in itself! I now recall one of the few sentences I had committed to memory as my siblings passed that family bible from one sibling to the next. These formed the tenets of Christian living I had learned at home. Thirdly, I recall an incident from another university: on the first day of class, the professor called the names of students enrolled in his course. Each student said yes when his name was called. He struggled at saying my last name, but I helped him. Then he asked "Are you sure you signed for this class? "Yes, Sir I replied. What he didn't realize at the time was that I had read his body language correctly. I was the only black student in that class. His body language said a ton of words to me. I studied my buns off to pass that class! I had learned to read body language. It's my hobby. You may have experienced similar subtle experiences in your personal life. Take courage. Keep on marching like a good soldier or Marine.

Psalm 71 verse 11 says "God had forsaken him: persecute and take him, for there is none to deliver him." When somebody tells me "No, you cannot do that," I tell them that is their opinion. I know who I am. Don't allow people to label you. Know who you are. You are a child of God. And God does not make any junk. HE is not going to abandon you or forsake you. Be comforted. Know that "He has begun great things in you, and He will see you through."

Chapter 17: Way Forward: Some Reflections

Many people ask me "How does it feel to be 80 years old?" I tell them my short answer: "wonderful." I could not have made it thus far without the Lord. Where would I be without you, Lord? In a dungeon of hell!

Seriously, any age is transforming. Particularly though, attaining age 80 is truly transforming. Why? It is because at age 80, God transformed me. He changed my "Impossible" to "My Possible." It is interesting to note the word "impossible" can be broken down into these two parts, namely "im" and "possible. "I split the word. I changed it into "I'm Possible."

I am amazed to say the more things change in my life the more they remain the same. Let me tell you what I mean. The foundations my parents laid for me early in my years remain the same decades later! They are still the foundations that sustain and keep sustaining me from age 8 or earlier to more than seven decades later!

Hallelujah!

I once heard a commercial on the TV, which says: "age is only a number." The woman in that commercial added: "but mine is unlisted." It made me laugh! Living beyond 80 is truly a blessing! The Bible promised the human lifespan as "three score and 10 years", AKA 70 years. Any age above 70 is a super blessing. Getting to age 80 is like I have reached the top of a beautiful mountain; now I can enjoy the magnificent vista of the surrounding valley and meadows below!

If at 80 years of age you are alive and in good health, you are a multi-millionaire. You ought to celebrate each day with your friends, your children and your grandchildren. Take the time to tell them how much you love them. Take a walk around. Your pace may be slow, and that is all right. Your memory may not be as sharp as it used to be four decades ago. And that is all right, too. Medical doctors tell us that the "average" person begins to suffer memory loss as early as age 35 to 40. Indeed, our human body is "fearfully and wonderfully made." Many people ask me: "What is your secret?" I tell them "Moderation." Do whatever you do in moderation. Don't take yourself too seriously. Laugh a lot. Eat healthy food. Exercise daily. I'm sure you have heard these suggestions many times. You know the drill. Stick to it. There is another side to aging gracefully. Let us flip the coin. I will tell you a true story. This 96-year-old went to the hospital for a "wellness checkup. His Nurse asked him: "How did you get to the hospital?' "What do you mean how did I get to the hospital, he fired back, defensively. "Of course, I drove. What do you want me to do? "Walk, take the city bus, or come by taxi"? The nurse sensed that this man was getting rather abrasive. My point here is "don't take yourself too seriously. Some of us Senior Citizens need to develop a humorous answer to questions that genuine people ask us when they try to admire us for how we look to them in our 80's and beyond. They mean no harm. By sharing with them your humorous answers, you may have blessed them. Everyone of us is called to a ministry. Yours may be "sharing a moment of your good life!

I was "blessed" to fly to London, United Kingdom (UK) recently, to visit my 85-year-old brother and his family. I purposefully planned it as a "surprise" visit but coordinated with my nephews and nieces. My nephew picked me up from the Heathrow Airport in London. I asked him to drive me directly to my hotel. The next day, my niece took me to where my brother was staying at the Royal Free Hospital, in London. Imagine this scenery when I arrived at my brother's hospital room. He lit up like a Christmas tree! His mouth was wide open, like the renowned tenor, Pavarotti, voicing out his powerful voice at a musical concert! He said to me: "Is this John?" Yes, this is John, your brother. I came to visit you from the USA." For the next five or so minutes, he couldn't take his eyes away from gazing at me! I visited him for six hours each day for one week in London.

What is my point in narrating all this? I'm glad you asked. First, I am saying to you my reader: spend quality time with your family. A surprise visit, a telephone call, a simple prayer, or a carefully penned letter will make their day. Just tell them how much they mean to you. Tell them how much they enrich your life. Tell them a joke. Laugh abundantly with them and watch them light up like a Christmas tree! Second, I am saying "include and remember the younger family members. Tell them where you have been. Where you are today, at whatever age, 70, 80, or 90, they will be. It's just a matter of time." Life is too precious. Life is too short. Even if you live beyond eighty, and well into the nineties, you are like a tiny drop of water which falls into a vast ocean in life. Savor each moment. Live today to the fullest, for tomorrow is not promised. The Bible says: "Give us this day our daily bread. Tomorrow is not promised! A wise man once put it into perspective when he said to me, "today is the tomorrow you worried about yesterday." How clever! Remember that!

Chapter 18: My Final Thoughts

I had a dream a few months ago. My younger sister, who had died at age 51, like my father suddenly appeared to me in that dream. She said to me: "brother, you know that our dad died at age 51. If you remember, I also died at age 51. I came to see you because I wanted to see how a man looks like at age 80. I hugged her. I said to her "God is good. What you see is what you get. PTL." I hugged her passionately, then she disappeared.

As I reflect on my 80th birthday I am amazed to say the more things change in my life the more they remain the same. Let me tell you what I mean. The foundations my parents laid for me early in my years remain the same decades later! They are still the foundations that sustain and keep sustaining me from age 8 or earlier to more than seven decades later! Hallelujah!

Questions I am Most Often Asked

Question 1. In a nutshell, how would you summarize your book? I am glad you asked. I came (to America. I saw (the lives of hard working Americans.) I learned (from Americans and the diverse people who have migrated to this Great Nation in search of a better life.) I failed (many times, I might add.) and I prospered. Question 2. You mentioned in your book, your mentors throughout your journey and struggle. Could you tell us more about those names you mentioned in the Acknowledgements section? My parents, who nurtured me and instilled in me and all my siblings a firm belief and trust in the Lord, no matter what we are going through.

My oldest brother, who loved all his siblings and encouraged us all the time. It is worth mentioning that he was the only one who had graduated from High School and had secured a job as a Customs Officer by the time my father passed in 1956. As in many families, the oldest sibling often had to take care of his younger siblings after the passing of a parent.

My maternal Uncle, the Late Chief A. E. A. Soremekun, who took me under his wings and paid my high school fees after my father had passed away in 1956.

My other Uncles and Aunts, who demonstrated it takes a village to raise a child in Africa, and perhaps in other parts of the world. My mentors, and they are many. I cannot list them all for fear I may not include the entirety. These mentors inspired me to excel, persevere, and continue to be who I am.

My wife, the Late Agnes Ndungwa Akinyemi (nee Muthiani), of almost fifty years. She demonstrated what true love can accomplish. My adult children, ADEDOYIN and OLUTOBI AKINYEMI, for their constant and unfailing love, trust, and belief in remembering and adhering to whose children they are. And lastly to my grandsons, Isaiah, Joshua, Randy Skipper, and Malik Skipper, for giving me a chance to "do it the second time and DO IT SO WELL."

Question 3. Can you tell us why you wrote your book, how you chose the title, and share with us what advice would you give to authors who want to become an author like you?

That is a multi-part question. I will do my best to address its various parts: I wrote my autobiography (the book) because I wanted to tell my own story. Nobody can tell it better than I can! If somebody else does, it becomes history, i.e., "his story." I wanted to write "my story."

I chose the title because I had just become 80 years old, going on 81, and joyfully aware (knock on wood) that I am now anticipating two more decades of life on this Planet Earth! Write now or forever hold your breath. I chose the former!

My advice to aspiring authors is as follows. Anybody who has lived a full life has something fascinating to share with the world. The trick to writing an autobiography is to treat it like any good story. It should have an author, you, a central theme, and a cast of fascinating characters to keep readers engaged. You may wish to think about a certain theme or idea that you have experienced in your daily life to spin your story around. Craft the story of your life in a story telling fashion as if your readers are walking with you along the way. Polish your writing to make it sing!

About the Author

I am Dr. John Ayoola Akinyemi. I am 80 years old. I was born at Abeokuta, the Capital of OGUN State, Nigeria, West Africa. Both of my parents were Methodist educators. I have eight siblings. All of us were blessed to have been nurtured by parents who believed in God and trained us "in all your ways, acknowledge God and HE will guide your ways."

I and my eight siblings received our elementary and high schools' education attending Methodist Schools in Nigeria. I came to the USA in 1963 after graduation, in 1960 from the Methodist Boys High School (MBHS) Lagos. Nigeria. I attended Aurora University, Aurora, IL where I met my wife, the Late Agnes Ndungwa Akinyemi, to whom I was married for almost 50 years. My father was the Late Joseph M. Akinyemi. My mother was the Late Chief Marion F. Akinyemi. I hold four degrees, namely, a BS with a major in Biology and a minor in Chemistry from Aurora University, Aurora, IL, a Master's Degree from Northern Illinois University, DeKalb, IL, a PhD degree from Howard University, Washington DC and a Master of Public Health degree (MPH) from the Bloomberg Johns Hopkins University School of Hygiene and Public Health, Baltimore, MD.

I retired from the US Federal Government in 2006 after serving as a Civilian for 27 years. I am an avid gardener. I enjoy dancing, singing, and writing. I recently wrote and published a biography honoring my wife, Agnes Ndungwa Akinyemi. The title is "Coming 2 America." I am currently writing my own Autobiography, entitled "BEYOND 80."

I have two adult children, Adedoyin Akinyemi, and Olutobi Akinyemi. I have four grandsons, Randy Skipper, 30, Malik Skipper, 27, Isaiah Akinyemi, 17, and Joshua Skipper, 14.

Acknowledgments

Posthumously, I acknowledge the following: my parents, the late Mr. Joseph M, and Chief Mrs. M. F. Akinyemi, my oldest brother, Sir. Emmanuel O. Akinyemi, my maternal uncles, the Late Chief A.E.A. Soremekun, the late Archbishop, the Reverend Dr. J.O.E. Soremekun, my wife, Agnes Akinyemi, nee Muthiani, and my first cousin, the late Dr. Samuel O. A. Soremekun, MD.

I also wish to acknowledge my adult children, Adedoyin and Olutobi Akinyemi, and my grandchildren, Randy Skipper, 30, Malik Skipper, 27, Isaiah Olutobi Akinyemi, 18, and Joshua Demetrius, 15 13, and Isaiah Akinyemi, 16, as of the writing of this autobiography.

Photo Section

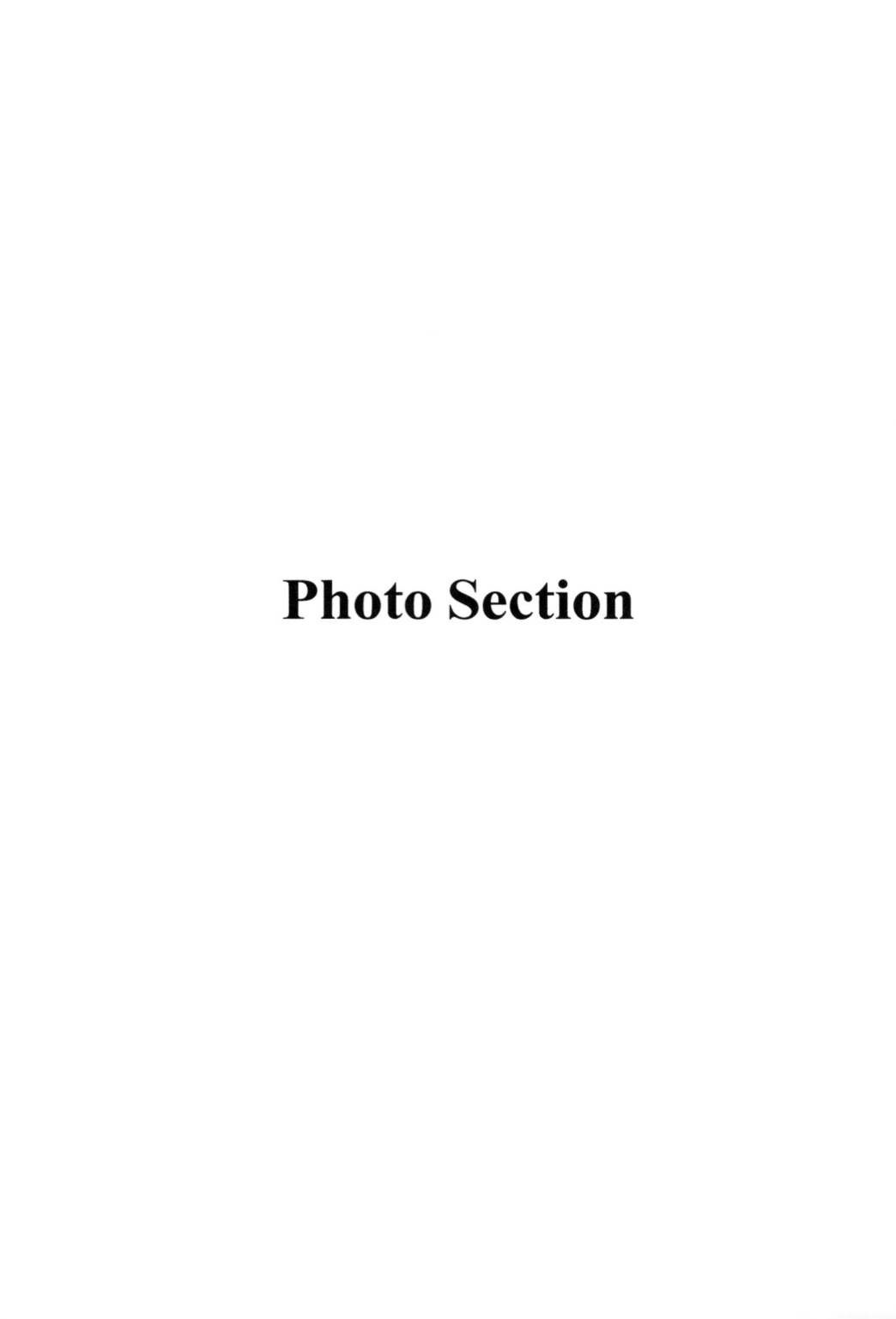

The last job I had before I retired, I participated as an Industrial Hygiene Inspector for the Marine Corps IG Program. This photo shows myself in Wake Island, one of the many places I visited for the Marine Corps.

This is my mother, the late Chief Mrs. M.F. Akinyemi. I owe everything I have learned to her. She passed away at age 87.

This is my late father, J.M. Akinyemi. He passed away at age 51.

My parents are shown together here.

My father and my oldest brother, the late Sir Emmanuel Obafunso Akinyemi. My father died in 1951, and this brother died at age 85 in December 2018.

Dr. John Ayoola Akinyemi

This is my father. On his lap is my oldest brother.

Beyond 80

This is my grandfather, the late David Aborisade Akinyemi. He lived to be 96!

This is my oldest brother, the late Sir Emmanuel O. Akinyemi. He was an accomplished organist, pianist, violinist, accordionist and choir director. He directed the choir 3 days before he passed.

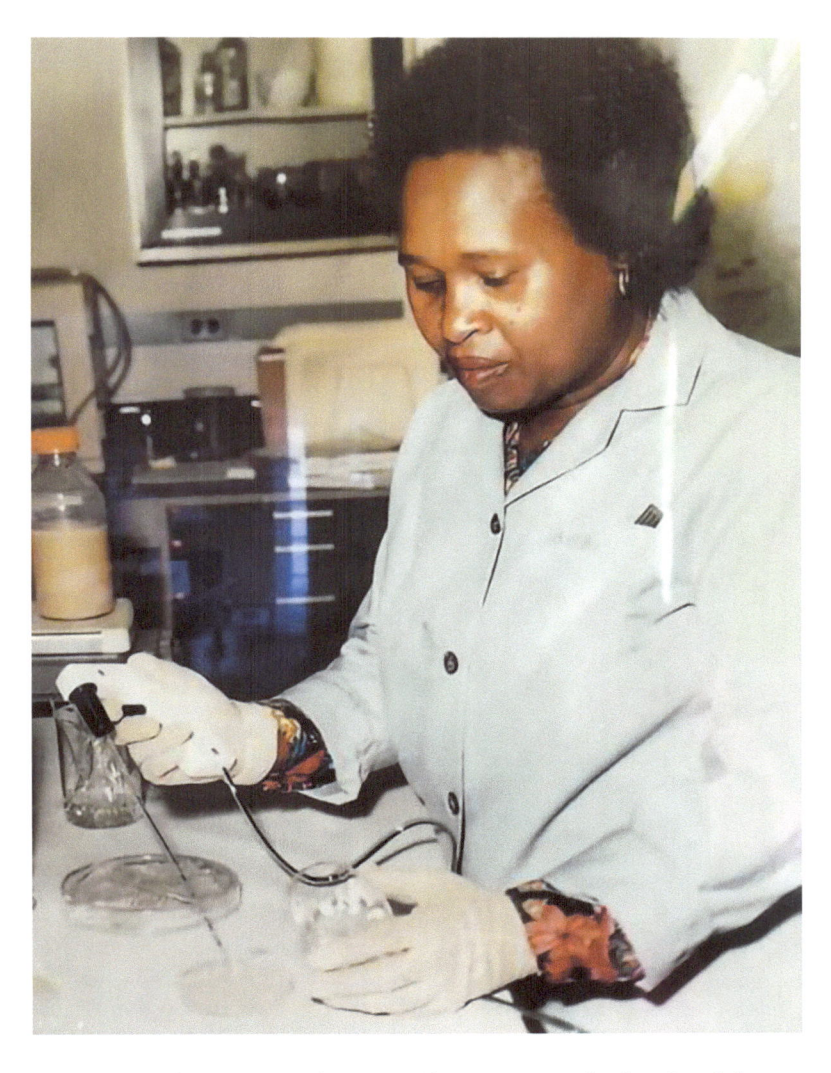

My late wife, Agnes Ndungwa Akinyemi, worked in her laboratory at the US Army, Aberdeen Proving Ground, Aberdeen, MD.

My parents and six of my siblings. Standing left to right are Emmanuel, Dad, Timothy is sitting on Dad's lap, Mom, my older sister Grace. Seated on the floor to the left is my immediate older brother Dele. Standing in the middle is my brother Olawale. I am sitting on the floor to the far right. This picture was taken before the last three siblings, namely Mercy Folasade, Bennett and Christopher.

Beyond 80

Agnes Akinyemi and daughter, Adedoyin Akinyemi in summer of 2005.

Dr. John Ayoola Akinyemi

From left to right, Agnes Akinyemi, Randy Skipper (daughter's husband) and Adedoyin Akinyemi in the summer of 2004.

Beyond 80

John with his cousin on his left, and a friend on the right in Houston, Texas.

John and his niece, grand-niece and grand-nephew.

My ethnicity is Egba, a member of the Yoruba People of Nigeria. This photo shows the National Convention held in Houston, Texas in 2022.

John and Dr. Bessie Soremekun, his cousin's wife, at the Egba National Convention.

Beyond 80

Shown with me here is Dr. Maurice A. Soremekun, MD

Five of John's siblings, and three nieces are shown in this photo.

Beyond 80

This is where it all started! My family and extended families!

Dr. John Ayoola Akinyemi

This is where it all began. My family and extended families took this photo on the dedication of my parents first home in front of 11 Alaba Street, Mushin, Lagos Nigeria, West Africa.